# tinderbox

dale winslow

*To Patrick,*
*Much Love,*
*Dale W*

NeoPoiesisPress.com

**NeoPoiesis Press, LLC**

2775 Harbor Ave SW
Suite D
Seattle, WA 98126-2138

Inquiries:
P.O. Box 38037
Houston, TX 77238-8037

NeoPoiesisPress.com

Copyright © 2013 by Dale Winslow

Dale Winslow – Tinderbox
ISBN 978-0-9855577-9-9 (pbk)
    978-0-9892018-2-7 (hardcover)
    1. Poetry. I. Winslow, Dale. II. Tinderbox.

Library of Congress Control Number: 2013916386

First Edition

Cover, design and typography: Milo Duffin and Stephen Roxborough

Printed in the United States of America

For Tom, Quade, and Harper

and to the poet who resides in us all

On the curve
of final question,
the wellspring
of innocent guile
satiates
the infinite helix.

# Contents

## (Un)Self

## The World

## White Noise

## Others' Light

# (Un)Self

## Tinderbox

I ignite, like the drunkard's match,
in exhausted alleyway at 2 a.m.
Ignite.
Burn my fingers on this fire
that strikes in hours deaf and blind.

I ignite, like winter kindling,
quickly and brightly as heavy scented cedar.
Ignite.
Rush of sap to open air, needle-rich,
heady release of earth and breath.

I burn, like birch bark,
written with welted words,
living pages of white set to flame,
these lines, smoke-signal reflections.
I burn,
and all that was, dissipates.

I burn, like ancient, peat bog fires,
memory, coiling and uncoiling,
a cryptic dance over moors.
I burn,
covering the moon with smoldering fingers.

I ignite.
I burn.
I ignite.

# Antechamber

Are you waiting in my antechamber?
Hidden there in the gathering of mosses and bark,
silent in the spilled-ink pools and bottled moonlight,
a slight shadow falling across your brow.

Among the sheaves of papyrus and promises,
endless rows of might-have-been proofs,
sepia-inked as the water about frightened squid,
these wave songs captured in half-sung sorrows.

Perhaps you are reclining in the hazy covers,
seeding phallic thoughts in the untouched spaces,
a finger pressed close to your lips,
a hush falling now as your palm touches
these confessional places,
now pensive, once impalpable.

I keep this room open for such things,
that cling to my sap-sticky life,
spider web scarves from distant woods,
tumbled stones from dead river beds,
the creeping ones with compound visions,
tinted sands of broken time and aching
breaths from obsidian reflections.

In my antechamber, ravens' shiny moments
and the mouse larder of strange obsessions,
spill over into scorpion-stung fruit.
The orchard's yielding tucked away here too,
fall and winter hoardings,
wizened thoughts of plentiful seasons.

My antechamber is very full –
I have spent my days and nights gathering,
and I dip endlessly into these treasures,
the black, the white, green and red,
all colours of life dancing on the walls,
fervent Kandinsky music and Dali dreams –

## Jazz

Through the amber lens,
I watch smoke coil its way
round my fingers,

the last knot of the day
complains its way loose.

In this couched life,
nothing remains
but the silken refrains
of magnolia scented song.

Sliding notes caress their lazy way
up my weary length,
and the sun sinks her failing smile.

I, in my somnolent blue,
dip deeper into this amber gaze.

Satchmo sings palettes,
and I dream a little dream
for me...

## Resolve

And you would hang it on me now,
softly severe,
the doeskin touch of this
comfortable discord against my skin.

And I would lean slightly forward,
in slow alacrity,
shoulders rounded, chin down
to take this breath-beaded weight.

And waking I would stretch to sky,
imperceptibly strong,
hazarding this heavy gift might slip,
revealing my vertebral curve.

## Riverbottom

When I stuck my hands
down there deep,
they trembled at the chill –
But the promise of
        smooth pebbles
kept them in
        until they ached.
The skin wrinkled up and I saw
        bubbles of white flesh
waiting to peel back and reveal
        raw, red promises.
I could not help myself.
I had to wade through.
Brushing aside the waterstriders –
    To my knees - so weak
            To my hips - so curved
                    To my breasts - so white
                            To my neck - to my neck
One coruscating pebble
set way down
called me,
and though my pockets were full already,
it convinced me to submerge –
and stay
Riverbottom.

## the humane holy

guardian of the hearth
squat under cedar arms
holding court
with shadows and ghosted fungi fear
my feet are bare
and make soft imprints
in the murmuring grass
i want to feel the earth
breathe under me
have that breath
move over me
and collapse all my expectations
grass becomes bare soil
and my feet are searching
cedar wraps itself around me
wisdom conveyed
in the language of scent
guardian calls me
i reach out in the pre-sun
something about g_Od losing itself
in the magnitude of this connection
flesh to granite
revelation coming
in flattened strokes
a curve in history
fire-womb markings
i lose place willingly
let go
and give something called
body
to forever
no punctuated explanations
there is no body
no soul
only this
which cannot be defined

## Wanting (Say it ain't so, Mr. Dawkins...)

It all comes down to wanting.
Whether it is the first breath of life
inhaled after fluid expulsion
or the last gasp fleeing on curled wave.

It is wanting that drives.
It pulls and pushes, it screams.
There is no respite from urges,
no Zen-like state that transcends
the basic force that drives the machine –
the flesh and blood, the bone and impulses,
an unconscious engine that races or falters on whim.

The mind that discerns itself apart,
is unfastened by its own logic.
In the end, there is only the wanting.
The end – the wanting lets go.

## What (knot) to due

I haven't made any
     lists yet —
I have been too busy
curling
   coiling
     as a snake
on fire.

I haven't made any
     lists yet –
of where they should sit
     *(the order)*
their elbow rubbing reconciliation

I haven't made any
     lists yet –
of which symbolistic wall to

paper
take down
or knock a hole in

*(a hole like the one in her unsmiling mouth)*

## Forgery

Signs catch you in
soft places

as you pass by
windows

flat shine
off your
life.

## At the End of Line, a Helix

From labour and thankless
wakening, the rooms become
warm, moving with the driven
insomnia of austere necessities.

Not still
          or clear,
animated by self
          deception

in the other flesh,
          orgiastic,
you have become

a clock for          parasites,

your time chosen by tongues

that have tasted
          the forecast
in Earth's          regress.

Clarity is eaten from the inside,
until nothing else can stomach
the brute, absolute vision
of inherited eviction.

## Anthropophage

Look under the skin,
dig your fingers in deep,
peel the dermis back,
fragile casing of meat.
Slip your hands into
the profound fibers of

>protein motivation
>ambulatory fascination
>suspended consummation
>degenerate exploitation

It's all the same when
slapped to Styrofoam
and wrapped in Saran,
the new transparency
stripped to white

>cellular constitution
>divided desperation
>recombinant violation
>genetic desecration

Bone dancer, you are the absent mind's
marionette, engineered to infinite
echo, the clatter of impossible movement.

## Infused Identity

i.

She says that when she first began this,
she was among those designated "mice".
She knows everyone here,
chats about their lives
as if they were family,
and maybe this is the truth.
Genetic flaws creating bonds
tighter than clan genesis.

ii.

There are 4, 6, 8 redemptions
packed into the bound book on the rolling table.
No flow and high scores are an issue.
The saline is a covenant,
a sterile sacrament.
Observances are made
at the sound of three short beeps.
The holy rites of medication.
The inevitable cycle,
recovery/relapse.

iii.

it burns
returns
like gin
to the source
something less direct
than memory
as if it were
the tears you dropped
last autumn
into the rain (pain) barrel
as you tried to wrestle the band
tighter

watching time
(which
looked like water)
trickle over the white
of your knuckles

## Impact

bed angled in the corner
this replicated in wide expanses of

glass
divided lines
(black)

cityscape
reflected in reflection
(escape)

rejection,
introspective caution
(boundaries)

*I case the mind in boneyard dreams*

bleached out
perceived perfection

transitional elation
smoking

paper sheaves edged in
life stream

*breath, blood*

thin slices slipping
wrist high

the scent of sex lacing
addictive li(e)nes about

*thighs, sighs, 2 a.m. cries*

release not reached
the pull of want borne by fingers
wishing only to be

*printless*

the realization that all is trompe l'oeil

brush strokes evident to the eye
shadows creating illusions
weathered patterns repeating

## Terms of Acceptance

she is no longer tied to
the pouring of life
she has become secure in
her mort-ality

she senses again the approaching
wave of death, and is pleased

*there is no shame in this*

she disregards her body and occupies her mind
with all provisional questions

*there are so few answers really*

living is far more simple than astonished
embodiment would suppose

*her attendant is not so easy with this contract*

transcendence shakes her by
the shoulders
pleads her away from the rape
of breathing

it seeks
    to capture
        to keep
            to own
                to end

but she, she has forgiven herself
the design of her imperfection
and she has grown ready

she runs prayers over her lips
until that well goes dry

*whispers of morphine mantras*

she waits
   she curses
      she begs

*her pain has become a blunt demand*

          still
        she remains
     and still
    she remains
   and she remains
 still

her attendant blessing the sun
even as death dances behind it.

## shift

Dali desires rend
the fabric of                    predic*tability*

what was, will not be      held
in hourglass                     grains
but wavers as heated      mirage

a constant quest<sup>ion</sup>
of sense and ill<sub>us</sub><sup>ion</sup>

opiate me
*aware*
strike me
*sent*ient

*I on eye*
     *say*
        *shun*

load the pistol
at my unmarked
~~starting line~~
cleverly shadowed as
~~finish~~

dark to dark
        blind

## instructions possibly included

if you create it
do so without
hesitation
set it surging
and unfasten
then and only then
will you safeguard
the option
of encounter

make sure to leave
a distinctive silhouette
in the jugular spray
one that might suggest
a spectre writhing
in strokes and arches

whisper
there is
more
there is
so
much
more

do not hide it in alleyways
slash it deeply open
in the exposed places
anywhere that life
plays you out
you bleed graffiti

you must leave
no signature
no modus operandi
only the Pollock grip
of a single bruised line

## The Waking Dream of Amnesia

Arriving
on each fallen beat
meeting the path
hardened by life-weight.

In the numeration
of g_Od,
you seek the inward flow of
cleansing.

In the future
of forgiveness,
you prey on the falling hands
of your ancestors.

Reverting, you become
hungry, driven
by blood whim.

In abandoned night,
you transpire,
sing flesh petals
over the stone
you would sleep beneath.

*filling forms*
*in an empty room*
*on a table that is inked*
*with names*
*that waited here before you*
*everything is in the waiting*
*the vital statistics*
*the coffee rings*
*the ashes*

*your fingernails*
*bitten to bleeding*
*you apologize for my inconvenience*
*hold the bitterness*
*of coupling on your tongue*
*pressing it tight against  your*
*soft, infinite palate*

## Accident

back-pedaling in this my
grey day
while stones fly in clattered dance
hands slick with the sweat
of decisions
and all this turning of wheels
their spokes lost in my mind
dust and summer heat
dry, choking
a tangled encounter of chain and limbs
as I fall
solo
from this bicycle built
for two

## Notes to the Almond Living in the Mind

Sanity does not leave all at once.
You find it in small spots scattered about the bed.
It falls off your fingertips as you pour coffee.
It scuttles under the floorboards to curl up with mice.

It says there is no reason to watch
other eyelids falling, that hopeless tangle
of flesh and fiber, binding and unwinding.

Sanity hides in the constant stretch of ticking hands
what goes on in the sprung arms of women and men
who discover pleasure in their own sensual decay.

There is no epiphany in falling away from obviousness,
in the ever-so-neat pleating of linen clothing
hung precisely over tenuous life.

There is no answered prayer or promised messiah
and not even your own godless religion can keep sanity
from running down the drain at day's close.

It sits beside you in the corner café and whispers
what you should eat, drink and how much to tip.

You leave nothing, and Sanity laughs.

## Just Short of Blue

A fallen integer
    of respect.
A typing
    of beginning.
An accounting
    of ending.

In the direction of your
desire
and the shadow of your split second
(coming)
you have buried the future.

In the stacks of photographic
evidence,
memory's exhaust
chokes your today.

You have become
a detached shadow,
a witness to the breaking
of childhood.

Your vision is something like this –

pinholes
shot through with metal
and broken fibre.

## Wood Ash and Water

Shadowed morning
turns paradise to nighttime blue,
as the planks of a broken bed
flex and moan
in memory of cycles
halted mid-turn.

Your fingers are bloodied,
bones in the spokes
of what you meant to say
but could not,
through a door held shut.

Shoulder-ache
of separation
sings the necessity
of hiding
all the pieces
that will not fit.

In the foundation that
you built,
are the skeletons
of your ancestry.
You apologize for wrongs
you never knew,
blame staining
your hands.

In the evening,
you find lye
in the soft white
of your nesting palms,
and kiss the welcome burn
into something that was once
your name.

## rogue dialogue

words    words
    words
have value when
you
go back
round them
square them
pierce them
with the sharp
of a hook
reel them in
real in them
until you say
    *O*
and your
lines
become wrinkles
creases askew
in the corners
of your mouth
and you cannot walk
without letters
falling from your
life

## Couched Unconscious

That's it, touch!

Even the rarest respond, opening
vulnerable,
releasing tenuous hold on
reality –

   (mine:yours)

conceptual convolution
evolving desperation
the clinging of heavy-headed
memory,

*you are a ghost
with one withered hand.*

Orchid fictions
splatter your loins
with poisoned memoirs.

You are in regression,
weeping,
your secrets half-peeled away.

You are on your knees,
praying
for the tapping to stop,

*ribbons about your wrists,
as if to hide the fear.*

## Seattle Mainline

Like sparks you fly
from narrow places and black pools,
holding inverted prism escape

pock-marked kisses of fine steel
competing like salmon on your arms.

You stretch out ragged embraces
in frenetic attempts at humanity.

You trace the skyline, and draw in
the blue and purple bruised air,

all this possesses your waking state.

Your breaking fate is shaking.

Eyes, set with fires
blazing crosswise,

opportunity turns to ash.

Tarmac life,
smoking ovals cloud the night.

This for you.

The last push available,
the funnel of worn-out life,
you screaming silent "O"
startled at your misplaced poise.

Another face,
receding against splattered night,
shrugs relief into opened veins.

This city siren is shrieking,
and foaming breath leaves nothing lit.

A final caress,
brutal and loving.

**undefined**

Are you going to learn
to pray?

This skin you're in
is playing
                vibrational
                        delusions.

Are you going to learn
to take care of IT?

this
spark –
        this sulphurous
                    stain,

        is strong enough to cost you
        ice    and    shame...

Across the mountain spine,
you leave your
        breathprints,

in the sky
you shutter your I's
against the glacial
blinding

Are you going to learn
to see?

These skies below,
are in striking
distance –

you hit the false
ceiling,
a soundless shattering
of I-mage

Are you going to learn
to fall?

Trust the smashing
of your
bones,

this     real-i-gnment
of your
soul,

trying to die this

one
        last
                death.

## the way you sound when you phase indefinite

you find the voices
deep in the back of your throat
they move up like monks
touching simply and in reverse
minding the sinful brainscape
of your accomplished misbelief

with deceptive concentration
thoughts skip and soar
they improvise the matter cords
stretching pliant tongue
and you speak with the flat groove on

you shift, sway, then float,
transportable as tomorrow things,
butterflies have no effect outside time
you dust for hypothetical God-prints
caught in the act of subtle conception

## (lucid:dicul)

We sleep in eggshell by day,
not knowing this to be slumber,
light pale in its transference.

We are categorically incapable
of shielding ourSelves from
the complaining slap of awake.

We stiffen, sunlit-calcified,
move minor, unknowingly deliberate,
our programming incomplete.

We do not flinch from cog-nizant swellings.
We are gears, regardless.

We wake in passing haze by night,
pinching phantom skin to painless
peaks and exaggerated blooms.

We pray for depth to butterfly deities
whose wings suspiciously bruise
the spreading, tired blue of our faces.

## Now as Before

How you felt at the beginning,
where you don't feel now –
dust trails over the lines you crossed,
sandstorms turmoil your soft tissue,
the places on your body blooming
with botfly's provisional promises.

The way you spoke at the beginning,
roe & milt spilling fertility,
the frantic division & multiplication
of choking conundrums,
the richness of overflowing verb(age)
scaling stains down your white shirt.

How you saw at the beginning,
where you are blind now.
fisheye complexities stretched
to taut impressions, reversed &
inverted in optical confusion,
mirror-hall options limiting/limitless.

## The Drowning of Dawn

*"It is an hypothesis that the sun will rise tomorrow: and this
means that we do not know whether it will rise."*
*- Ludwig Wittgenstein*

*How the storm settles only under her eyes.*

How you know the spot where her spine curves in
    and exactly the pressure that eases it.

How you open the silk drapes in the morning,
    let in whatever the day offers, declare it good.

How, between the voices of people who judge your soles,
    you draw small spirals in corners of unread notes.

How the ink is always black
and the spiral always clockwise.

How you wait until the traffic is gone
    and watch the sun settle its face into the sea.

*How you wonder if the sun can drown.*

How you walk by rows and rows of empty desks
    and enter numbers which make people feel safe.

How in the parking lot you see only one car,
    only one way to return.

*How you wonder if you should simply walk.*

How you open the car door, slide behind the wheel
    the engine turns over, nothing else seems to move.

*How the road slips from under you and your eyes
are immaculate.*

How the storm falls down her face and into your palms
    as you hold her and know there is no boundary.

How the sun *did* drown without you knowing,
    this is the last time the day will end.

*How the night goes on forever inside shared breath.*

## notwithstanding convictions

in the fall and rise
in the desire for something
you believed would come
but never did
you find the currency
of response
there is an echo in nature's corridors
that belies solitude
and embraces
the diminish of green

*therefore*

you have water and words
and the flow
reaches out to a bearing arm
something positioned
beneath sleep
and your fears
strings of lost phrases
forgiving intonation
the last unified thought

## i am

molecules moving through
the stained sun's faded hairs
curling inward

memories set upon
themselves
refusing release

bundles of light erupting
all about the house

remindersechoesreflections

yellowed edges crisping
from time's sweaty touch

once twice three times
about the room then back
molecules moving through

once     sun's creaking smile

twice     dancing green and blue

thrice     forgiven

## crossed wires

it is ending
yet never begun

this slight flicker
a light bulb, blown out

with one touch,
such a faulty switch

## Disambiguation

Oh! So easy riding the war horses!
The freezing men and hungry dogs
profound in their blood feast
proclaim victory in harsh winter night.

They are lost in consuming the controller,
ammunition passing beautifully through rigid forms.

No breath is honestly lost.

Dismal, Mr. Dismal, long and reading to me
as I type his offspring thoughts.
Stripped and starving, we commit pleasure crimes
against the dying world.

Trembling child/man, locked liar,
collared master of prosody and passion,
I dig the deep grave that will bury us both.

This is deafeningly profound.

As of and never read, heard now as this, yet only by
your ears, in time provided by someone else's breath

I seek these moments of insight.

Proviso! Proviso! You have some obligation
to transport me elsewhere.

I am neither love nor
     hatred
but simply and suddenly
     ended.

## Unshackling

The complication of the animal
breaking out inside you
tears down twisted absolution.

You seek out the scent of union,
sightless perfection
consummated by loam and rain.

In the expansion of eye you find
the domesticated suspended
and perch on the edge of satiation.

You move through the delicate
fracture of space made by fingers
seeking the plush of parted time.

The silence after Thunder speaks
to the indifferent beauty of Itself.

You let
go.

# The World

## Playground Parity

It's as simple as
skipping rope Peppers,
faster, faster,
becoming encased
in the blur
of pink crossovers.
It becomes binding,
ties you,
trips you,
one long strand, knotted
without purpose.

It's as complex as
Double Dutch,
left, right,
jumping swiftly
between the two,
finding rhythm
in the opposition,
knowing that
to favour one
is to lose them both
and so moving
becomes essential.

It's as innocent as this,
as intricate.

## List Price

it is as if
in this window
there is something
not quite worth
the tag amount

resale inevitable
the profit slim at best

value calculated on fingertips

counted here
1 2 3 4 5

and again here
1 2 3 4 5

like schoolyard riddles
and kaleidoscope visions

cryptic
hypnotic
beautiful

obscured

## rise, not dawning

sun running
reptile abandon
over hills
trees raped
in silhouette
days ingested
as minor chords
weeping colours
held in eyes
abandoned by river's
dry bed anguish
racing to the east
never finding source
all this movement
brings no grace
waking in ditches
along misplaced roads
      you should have left long ago
      you should have burned the evidence
      you should have worshipped your fall
          you should never have woken up

## Mountain Woman

I travel up Mountain folds to where
she births between her ridged thighs
sighing wings and misted ice.
She has pushed them out to meet me,
I, damp from the embrace of her tears.
In my hair and silvering my lashes,
are joys and sorrowed remembrances.

A single, scaled flicker follows my trail.
The high paths are slicked to icy sheen.
I run quick and sure-footed to the forest edge,
the wolf leads the way in the hummock spread.
The span of my fingers across my eyes
splits the sunset into scratched brilliance.

In the shadowed wood I see
hunched Raven Man.
He calls my unspoken name,
the sign of inside sight.
He draws me out in the crusted white.
He wants to kiss my lips, leave
a frozen blue stain upon their arched top.
It is the moon mark, the sign of
wild ways remembered.

The winter speaks to him, crinkles
the lobes of his fungus ears.
He bends to the bitter, chilled words
and drops his teeth onto the snow.
They burrow in the banks of sleep
and he turns to me, raising
feathered arms wide and cries out,
gums bleeding the pain of ancestral loss,
a coiling sage-smoke breath, bleak dreamscape
of burnt stumps and dying salmon.

Mountain Woman, where is the path?
Where does Raven Man dissolve into
the sharp-needled black of forest?
Mountain Woman, there is bark left to gather
and a mad, wrathful basket to weave.
It will catch the spiked embers that fall
into your rocky flesh folds.
You bleed smoke to cover Raven Man.

Oh! Mountain Woman, do you see me?
Settle your heavy-lidded stare on my face,
hood my restless spirit with Raven's wings.

## Antidote

Water snake, you slide between my thighs
and the driftwood fork of you
beds splinters in my flesh,
there is no recourse for this action.

I trace the pattern of these dead things,
pleasant punctures of serpentine grace,
sharp arrows of self-righteousness.
Quilled, I slip down, spine to stone,
send my hands trailing
liquid fingers to the riverside.

All winter you slept under me,
coiling, uncoiling,
torpor ridden and ice-burned.
When the green shoots split your sides,
you woke hungry for the river,
and twisting out, threaded your sinew
through the stones.

Water snake, you sprout legs,
slowly they emerge, unfold,
as waking spiders, each a jointed
complaint to your belly.
You scuttle sideways, rolling
hardboiled eyes at drowning moon.

Touching the current,
I take up the water line,
gather it to my breast and swallow
this hot pebble left on my tongue.
You flounder in the rippling
spider twigs scrabbling against
your demise's red scales.

Under patient moon, I pull out
each peculiar fragment,
plant them on the shore.

They bud skitterish legs
and weep themselves
into the mossy night.

I touch my fingertips to
these raised welts on my thighs,
cover them in spruce pitch and ashes.
This life blood smoldering,
I release, cup the open sky.

## InSights

*There is a sniper in the forest,*
*crosshair dreamer, high up*
*in the between spaces.*
*A predator, a broken*
*hermit testifying,*
*a cynical minstrel spilling*
*fruitful ammunition.*

You are on the path.
You take snap shots
using insect vision.
Caught colours creep, seep
into your flesh. You are
camouflaged and leave your
scent as testament of passage.
You break the day's egg over
your brow and do not flinch.

You are at the cliff.
You prowl edges, alive,
discrete and brightly vacant.
You seek the salt of sea, which
is nothing like blood, nothing
like breathing, nothing like
your molten mind. You touch,
you soften, you try to dissolve.
You have found gravity, you
beg(in) consequential echoes.

You are kneeling.
You pray, exposed on the rocks,
weeping colours from your skin,
you surrender to life, to the cross
+haired, sharpshooting song
of harvester, to the quiet
weapons of awareness.

You are bending into the ache.
You descend violet and green,
breathe black, bloom white,
you are water shadows, you
are humus heat.  Slipped serpent
blindfold retreats and your eye,
burrowing pinpoint, dilates awake.

## Slopes and Feral Freedom

Zippered scars mark her steep breasts.
Up the streaked sides they go, wanting
unity with her, but divided still.

The babble of metal beats the echo.

Sun's eggyolk heart is pierced,
weeps buttered light upon
the white nakedness of earth flesh.

The core bones lie exposed.

Flurried light dances, refracted.
The distracted crowd surges,
rides on scars, past the eyed forest.

Almonds of wild memory watch.

Drunken life goes downhill.
Silence descends, I creep out
onto clouded hills and walk alone.

I taste the trail, paths marked
by animal feet. Feral freedom
purifies me and –

I crave the overtaking of my cultivated nature.

## viviparous estuary

this is the     first way   it was:
*high*
     *volume*
         *rapids*
white swell pushing you
     into
adrenalin shock

     *(jolted opal)*

it was electric surrender
the hard snap of verb
set loose among
the many aspects
to be revealed.

certain shades urge
sodden blessings to crawl
over rocky shores.

outcry is left
as small drops
on the
smooth
blue
of otter skull.

**FearLess**

Each way I am
apprehended
fingers in brambles
as hummingbirds speed
to their thimble nests
quick and oblivious
to their hearts which quiver
at such speed they should

                                        stall

and perhaps they do

up there

        at top

             of arc

where     they     hover     briefly

then
plummet
fighter-jet
free

fearless of thorns
which have caught me
in scarlet rich sting.

## Press Return

He wants to access the code
and determine the source.
He wants to embrace the pain
found somewhere beneath his
right temple.

> *a sign a string an explosion*
> *of p.articulate dread*

Discontinuity creeps into his slow,
cold bed while he lies naked
on the bathroom floor, embracing
pure white syringe detachment.

> *everything is shades of static*

Insects tell him hives are built from
the perfect geometry. A lotus/locust
emerges with answers, parasitically seeding
the hemispheres with the numbers of
shattered heaven.

## Without Landmarks, Without Sky

The day was moving in moss
and his success came measured
by the distance he travelled in her.

He kept the compass to his right,
turning her over to the left.
Mounting from behind,
he maintained perfect direction.

He moved the hinges of her spine
and in her flexibility, discovered
his shoulders humming.

He missed her more
when he was with her.

He imagined she had
no direction at all.

He moved the compass, watched
the needle bounce, his success,
the moss, his eyes loose.

Years ago, he felt the compass
move from deep inside her.
Back then, he knew about polarity.
He extracted and reversed it.

He will not remember this place
and it will not remember her,
Anemoi ridden.

## Architecture, Archetype

This is the written law,
set loose in the storm of your words,

the dark-horse violation and collapse
of imperfect society, the pall
of fabricated civilization.

Every cornerstone is faulty.
Every mason is faulted.
Every symbol is wanting.

A sandstone promise erodes
in the inevitable dripping of time's water,
the grains of certain downfall.

No logic will hold this together,
a compounded fracture of weakness.

And so we take lovers,
many and varied, seeking
that element lost within ourselves,

three-fold, intimacy, knowledge and compassion,
done quick disservice in the thick incense
of hierarchical construction.

The temples are as diverse
as the beds we have shared.
Words bruise that which we seek.

And always the written law,
building walls about our awareness.

## The Words Behind Your Words
*for Si Philbrook*

The third winter,
there was betrayal
and a falling Lark-
in meeting the slant
of modern creation –

an effigy of Love's sublimation.

Here, a touch of mercury
where sorrow etched itself,
bright and naked,
into a song, possessive
of cruelty and return.

Fondled memories,
thick-tongued
in passion, lick
themselves clean,

content in capitulation.

The fourth winter,
vacancy
and remnants
of some further
forgotten summer.

## so the spirits will know him

after his scarification,
he found a high hill.
here he had to bury
his bloodied bandages,
so that this part of him
would remain
near the village.

through the rain,
his energy would move
into the ground water,
and so, it would flow
over the lips
of the children –
vision of the future.

in the hut with green walls,
he is offered fresh milk
and the flesh
of clean-spirited animals.
he is assured
that the ancestors smile down
on the bond he has made.

in this village, on this hillside,
there is no web but the one
cleared away from a corner.
there is no vanishing,
no need for written language.

## Splinter Fish

Splinter fish swims carelessly,
a fish bone for a hook,
irony and devastation.  The hook
is hidden and consumed,

it becomes familiar with the throat
of the consumer.  It becomes an issue,
a whispered confession of excess.

Such is the way with things
organic and mathematical,
abundance, famine, the gauche
gestures of life choking.

## On the Thin Street

On the thin street
the tin can is silent.
Straw-prickled scarecrows
spin on sticks,
and a rustle of newspaper
keeps life
lit and burning.

Another tooth falls
and rolls in the gutter.
Greased wheels turn
silent and complete,
but life is a shuffle
of bent cards
by stained fingers.

A ragged day paced out
in calloused time.
Bottled blues buzz
in the air,
a twitching lip
finding green
displeasing.

Night brings
sharp-edged smiles.
Shattered laughter
rings the satin neck.
Curls of smoke choke
joy's fresh breath.

On the thin street
the tin can rattles.
Cards twist free
and the sloping
back of crippled day
carries night in pieces.

## D (diminished)
*for Stephen Morse*

(doh)

Turning under,
the green becomes
something
more,
a potential,
the uncertain rescue
from sunlight.


(ray)

Slanted,
at times finding its way
between the places
where skin cannot slip –
one cell at a time.


(me)

Somehow,
more is coming away,
always another inside
or outside or even
    apart  i-n
  d.v.ne
d.v.s.on
  d.vers.on
    (which am .?)


*(fah)*

*It's not so very far,*
*by undercurrent.*

(soh)

~~mended by the erosion~~

(lah)

A singular rounded moment
opening,
causes even the
strongest gravity
to become
elastic.

(te)

If you could
read
what lies at the bottom
circumspect in silence,
would you?

(doh)

Beneath is not
less than above,
one vibrating moment
into another.

## Presence

*Vibration, translation –*
held moment fluttering
a million wings
as time tears itself apart
and sings electric waves
through corporeal things
  *– intimate, immediate.*

*Migration, transformation –*
the eye of one sees clearly
the other held just so
and inward draw of breath
proceeds out through mouth
opened to OM oval
  *– distant, transcendent.*

## Broken

I wake to morning suffocations,
a rancid choking of
yellow fog and curdled milk.
I slice my finger and
strawberries fall to the tiles.
This has all happened before.

Open the window –
A bird hits hard
and lies crooked in the ivy.
I swear I saw that
poppyseed eye roll,
accusing me.
I am to blame.
I turned the handle
to let the air in.

I bind myself with vines
and lie beside this
winged body, warm
as fresh-baked muffins.
I and bird are angled.

There are boot prints on the bed,
keys rusting in the rain,
and moss in my mouth.
The sky collapses,
pushing us both
underground.

## The Script of Mind

They are only interested in
whether he can tell a story,
make them feel something or
regain what that they have lost.
They will give him stars, oceans
and the finest room in the house.
His picture will have A-ranking
and sell on the interest
surrounding it.

They tell him what the story will be,
slowly bring the margins in
close to his skin.
They admire his heart,
take it out and watch it expectantly
while he presses the keys,
reads the curves and rejects
the audible distractions.

> Through the walls
> he hears
> a man crying,
> wonders at his line
> of work
> or whatever led him
> to break apart.
> He wonders if this kind of damage
> can be insured.

> There is nothing common
> about this man
> and yet everything ordinary
> is contained in those tears.
> He edits away the edges
> of the man's story
> and makes it his own.
> The paper remains    blank.

On the wall, time peels away
the paste of some-year.
He waits for an indication
that his words are not
regurgitated social lubricant
while he imposes favours
on wrestled affections.

He is infected,
remains singular in interest,
wears his passion as hidden images
and looks for opportunities
in each moment
of what he sees as
a straightforward drill.
Broken by bottle and ego,
he builds the walls back up
to evade the commonality
seeping into his bed.

The man shows him the moves,
pins the pain directly
on floorboards and fabric.
They lift each other fluidly
and compare body to mind,
both blocked in their own way,
each fraudulent,
each hanging hopes
on the kind of heat
that leaves without saying goodbye
and returns without knocking.

Take after take after take,
they are thrown
against the ropes
as language fails
and paths are worn
to no particular destination.

## Dog-eared

This is the portrait of times.
This is the blessing of stitches and gauze.
This is the undoing of plastered walls.
This is the burning of the craven gods.

Backwards walk down open throats,
a pustule of boiled promise edges the lips,
fingernail's dragged tip splits
the tidy seam of daytime veils.

Intestinal bracelets and arterial paints,
all the red spilling like crushed strawberries,

And the floor is slick.
And the day is long.
And the boots hit cemented moments.

Dog licks the juiced insides clean.

## There Will Be Time

Around the abnormalities
of afflicted metropolis,
gas-lit halos brighten
the blurred edges of a dirge
scratching at the horizon.

*And they come with*
*painted arms,*
*disturbing time,*
*the reversal of knowledge,*
*morning knowledge*
*of spoons and burning sugar cubes,*
*of what paints itself*
*in the back streets and rented rooms,*
*with arms to hold onto*
*all the Arms that wrap and crack.*

There is a beginning here
at the narrow end of things,
where loneliness leans out
of the shuttered day
and all is uneasy peacefulness,
mouths stretched to breaking
and broken so, find no profit
or prophecy in their damage.

*After the fade,*
*after trailing of fingers*
*across the brow,*
*there is a pause in night's progress,*
*dusk, temple to the illusion*
*of three-dimensional space.*

Over the River, life
melts to tender grandeur,
Turner bleeding light
into impressions of earth as heaven.
It is here the spectrum is smudged
so very sanctimoniously
behind the imagined freedom
of distorted focal length.

## Binary Sacrifice

Thou shall/shall not
plant the green now
under the vast red fields
of yesterday.

Thou shall/shall not
concatenate your
hesitant blue hope
with the illusory yellow
of rebellious tomorrow.

Thou shall/shall not
cast your nets while
the remorseless sea
consumes the land she
shamelessly touches.

And thou shall/shall not
deny her expanding arms
and her arrogant repose
of perpetuity.

Thou shall /not/knot
each other to forgotten promises
and read among the bones
of oracle bitch the supposed fate
of your uncompromising religion

## Title

You have to hit them with a hammer
if you want them to stay until
the end of the performance.

People take such pleasure in the denial
of comprehension.

*Note to Selves: there is no Messiah*

unless
 he is wearing
 a white t-shirt
 a leather jacket
 smoking Gomorrah Camels
Light

There is high tension in the
towers of Babel.

Choppers shadow the desert
and you begin at 30 seconds
 counting back,
some unseen hand turns the
hourglass again and starts
the falling time-sand of
rationally repentant people.

He has buried their prayers and passions.

Remember this is just the prologue,

Wait till the intermission –

The signal,
signing the package
delivering white lies.

It's at the address.
It's under the postmark.
It's in the spit sprayed over the covering paper.

  Open it!
 They will admire you for your
    lack of connection.
They will admire you for your
    disturbed recollection.

It's all wrathed up now
in vague envy.

"Vengeance is mine."
said the Lord of some-bodies.

## After Your Hours

Sick, thick
ripping rock n' roll,
wet mouth wide with
why's
and the wet undress
of thighs spreading.

One broken cheekbone
cradled in scarlet
suspension
over early morning
asphalt.

They are cutting the
grooves
in rude, raw rush
amidst hush of
impassioned
insecurity.

There are fresh warnings
posted,
some minor-key violence,
your satisfaction is
arrested
and no one has been killed.

Hit me up with
metronome modifications,
slam these blistered
resurrection riffs
way over there, on
Salvation's last stinking
island.

## any other road being the same

outside a grainy wisdom,
the highway
pencils regression
between covers
yet to be found.

in Brando white,
there is a simple plan
formulating
under the guise
of eastern routes.

something spills from the head.

travels become
inked in the flesh.
Charley knew.

and Sal left his sweat
on the fortunate mile
that ended it all.

## Steve's Stage Combat

Some stages are
        slippery.
You have to break
        your fall
while looking at
        your belly.

*(head off the ground,*
*fall to sitting down)*

Hands martial the break.
Lathering.
Loathing.

*(It's all in the technique...)*

Hitting
without a mark,
Choreographed Conflict.

In this way we may emerge
        unscathed,
and perhaps, if we are
        fortunate,

*survive.*

## Mémoire sans Soleil

As it began so
it stopped,
folding into itself
accordion finger handcuffs,
a strategy that spoke
of the limitless possibilities
outside the line drawn
by solar birth.

He said the warplanes
would one day break through
the Father's womb wall
and in the clanging hypnosis
of iron bells,
the dancers would ride tiptoe
on wooden ships
crossing vast seas
of sometimes, forever.

He spoke of hands
held up and outstretched
in never-ending supplication
to archetypes and histories,
counting ten the days and nights
of humanity's demise.

In the dank of the dockyard,
fishermen scrape galaxies
from the sides of ancients,
a gift from beyond graves
the beds of sleeping tomorrows.

Little children name each falling star
as they lift it from the earth
to rest in the heaven of their fingertips,
whorl upon whorl and the rings
of ages winding themselves tight
about all those given transient form.

He spoke spirals of cities,
the wheels of roadways rotating
verbs and advertised curiosities
about the broken cemeteries  nestled
between the breasts of halted birth.

In this action, He scripted the essence,
lifting the entire wired world
with one hydrogen kiss,
replacing with mushroom bloom
the peeled face of humanity's horror.

Her eyes open,
His eyes open,
watching as much
as being watched,
if not more.

Frame after frame saved
on the sacred skin of all our children,
our people in every appearance
impermanent as ink.

Hiding hypocrisy
in a code which is the message,
an absolute revealed
by its hiding.

Industrial curiosity falls weary
on ravaged lands,
on people tied to lineage
and some perception of longevity.

The walls between
are thinner than rice paper
wet in summer rain,
the burnt offering of one
leaves its scent in the wake of the other.

He tells me there is no
earthly paradise
either to be found
or lost,
in two ways the violence will
bring down time.

In the opening of vision
and the out-breath of animism,
every fragment of creation
will release its visible
counterpart and unwind
in the broken temples of man.

So it was in the beginning
and now as in the end,
in this possibility,
this particular closing of eye.

# White Noise

## letters from white noise

domesticated death
sliding this lid
peering at
birds
uttering a
reversion falcon
opening to
empty
and there is
no poetry
coming
and then
more amore
your sadness
sung
in the closing universe
and you stamping
my singular breath


among us
you deliver
shear cutting
with exotic walking
I remember Lord
your false fire
your frozen repentance
the ages of doorways
hidden
blackness
the bareness of tunnels
and certainty
of reformation

I am in the white
coming at You
leveled
in the perfumed dawn
it is a steep climb
to early morning
clusters of
cyanide scent
your footprints
shod and struck
this is the death
of soft expression
the praise of
words and
melody
You were
simplicity
and I was
Yours
in my complex
understanding

Wheels+
flags
we try and try
and still we are
old
dying
unanswered in
calling
there is no
eye
recognized
the blue pain

of fear
ending
and suddenly
stopped
we are not
we are
we

⌒⌒

subtraction
a warning
Our final
window looking out
over fallen Eden
Our change
to fawning conception
an awkward
lowering
I see now
more
than I did before
death
before
fear
You are my
opposite
side effect
I direct You
down
and We lie
in final
rest

## white noise from the coroner's cough

they like you torn
at the true
there is worse realization
arriving in boxes
stored in garages
arising from beautiful
suburban tragedies
two inches of mold
about raw buckled
years and the shout
of broken poetry
just before dawn
gurney love
hailing itself alive
and washing its feet
in a swill of deep
impersonal adulation
the speed of white
swoon
the rape of shrinking
souls
cold sun descending
on the waking body
gallows kiss
in the warm linen of
dark habits

## white noise from one future

she will push him over the edge
the one he walks around
cunt horizon frown
on a cocky bastard son
there is flesh on the floor
he, full on knife thrusting
she, taking the blade deep
and morphing it
lizard tongue recapitulation
there is a mutilation
waiting to be born
the offspring of source
and consumption
there is a price tag
hanging from its jaws
as it emerges
motionless
a stillborn delusion
of commerce and progress
everywhere are fluids
of desperation
and unrepentant wallowing
she will push him over the edge
into extinction's clinch
this love affair of humanity
this fucked and sightless trust

## white noise from electroshock echoes

insanity
fed in pill portions
by filthy nurses
with secret Freudian smiles
null and void
breathless and insomniac
flowering
a year, an hour, a minute, a second
no activity and
no opinion except
the vacancy of temple activity
boarded-up windows
where missing sights rest
and dead feet go
shuffling beat to collision, clash,
therapy mustached
the canary's demise
the contusion of sunrise
inspecting the squalor
of mind's impregnation
with a squealing mass of naked rats
aborted, abandoned, absolution annulled
by a blistered kiss
from a broken whore
disimpassioned
disjointed 24 hours
tic tock tic tock
pissed life running over
the bleeding sweet heart
left long ago
on cold, tiled floor
overdosed and overlife
the rickets of time
bowing memory to fecal knowledge
cheap seats to the play of days

contained in tight caresses
Clockwork, Clockwork
winding down thrusting
the one final disaster

## white noise from bukowski's empty glass

begging in deviant pinned alleyways
the broken pastor weeps
for another hit
palms bleeding
licks sneers from passing sheep
backway motel hell
an overflowing ashtray
the model of past persuasion
oleander promises
traffic pale running
across the window
your eyes fixed
on the hollow left in the pillow
a holy ill-fated impression
of love's forgotten scent
memory of taxi brakes
and jammed headlights, adulation
poor patron of abandoned breath
there are no miracles to wake the day
in the night, bread is broken
like the bones of a woman's face
bruised blessings kissed
from a clenched fist
a religion that always
brings them to their knees
in tears
  in sweat
    in tongue
      in cum
        in blood
and splintered dreams
laughing Buddha
embraces the herds of dawn
and the world slouches carelessly
into forgotten corner bars

## white noise from between nowhere

see the distance between
see it as nothing ever was
see it as an endangered void
the dimension where
time is not a factor
the equation limitless
and limiting
variables
constant
the affirmation
is
that if observed
closely enough
that final piece
holding g_Od
will emerge
*not Life though*
*Life is part*
*of the equation*
*go beyond*
*the mathematical*
*abstraction*
*to access*
*this final*
*code*
(is it a code?)
(yes.)
A Code of Silence.
this is why
they do not
Speak
those in the
Know.
there are footsteps
up
the mountainside
something
should have been

left
in the snow
but instead
is the sublimation
of distinction
and
defining
the journey
excludes destination.

## white noise from naked mr. burroughs

he tells me
it derives from the
absolute ventriloquist
in the dead of night
you know, like when you
have a dummy
who talks for you,
presents you as an introduction
to the first page of your own
life
it teaches speech
from abdomen
to lips
with a frequency that hits you
where you can't hold it together
you turn it loose
thick and revolting
a carnivore novel
consuming page after page
of pulp madness
in ancient speak
and this language
tosses out broken teeth
sprays spittle
drunken over your lap
kisses the screams to sleep
silences the conscious mind
with undifferentiated transparency
becomes burning oracular growth
of your elapsed other's wooden face

## white noise from a gunshot

what to see
what to do
only now to wonder
at the death
the depth
at the strangle
of understanding
a peeling dark
down the earth
shadows have seeped
into the ruin of your struggle
body bags are packed
for broken journeys
under the silence
of empty wells
something must
mean something
to an executioner
executing  the rhythm of
a revolver stopped
one spin short
bullet loving the barrel
kissing the warm temple of
flesh tasting time
leaving the metallic flavour
of one last clear thought
before breaking
into cellular jigsaw memories
one open mouth
singing alone
in a vacant dancing hall

## white noise from a funeral

you look up
smell their grief
and weep life
into the exaggeration
we call death
you try to make sense
while sitting on the
split rails
faith+fenced
and frequently going
into the aisles
wanting to give up
the difficulty
called living
confident in the deception
delivered by blood
inhaling the vinegar
of shortened experience
you cry up
and fly out
their grief holds you
inexhaustible
transcending contradiction
you smell of their sorrow
and bite your lip
birth invisibility

## white noise from ward 3

no words
no letters
only canvas unpainted
dark backlit shape mover
selling unknown quantities
of pain(less) flesh
intricate mechanized
collector of detritus
found down there
between the beds
and tall steel poles
scuttle ravenous in the blear
of quaking no-night
shiver slips to funnel womb
Mantis ready
its prayer
whispered
from beyond the other side
of yellowed shifts
in spectral swirl
embroidered eyes peer
roll to white
turn over the night
to seeping half-sun

## white noise from the world's stage

not remembering
the name of it
the title
the reward
the application
he puts it on
thinks out
moves all his thoughts
to the place
that will be protected
he calls it
and it comes
to him alone
slowly
he speaks it
aloud
to any audience
that might find him
he waits
for the floods of winter
buries himself
in withered growth
an immersed rattle
thinking
she might return
this thought touching him
as a wisp of air
to his mouth
it keeps him alive
in the torpor of autumn
his heart
a geode
of undetected splendour
his future
an uncertain wish
of erosion
hoping that
a wild river
will take his words
to her ears

## white noise from the network

they want their rage articulated
on screens throughout
the levels of their existence
there is division in the budgets
and stillness of deficits
they want someone to be
accountable
to hold heads over the fall
speak in the tongues of the masses
they want to be associated
and announced
they want reasons to go on
living, dying
they want to know that somewhere
a weapon is aimed
at the slaughterhouse they sleep over
they want imitated autonomy
with screen names that modify
their fetishes to defined levels
of acceptability
they are detached, dispassionate
and resigned
they wake to simpleton voices
that tell them truths they do not want
tiny translated armageddons
threading themselves through
wavelengths of altercation
in immune night they are cleansed
of ideology
in the recession wilderness there is no
hidden value
only madness and protestation
there is barking out the windows
as dogs find their voices
the electron temple
resonates with sound-wave idiocy
half-truths spilled in
packaged programming
gospels of cable and contortion
delusional tube feeding
and between input and output
they never hear a sound

## Nothing About the Table at All

Challenge the
supposition
that you
are adept.
There are thresholds
to step over
or hit up against
to see if they
inhibit you.

From impression
to detection,
from The One
to The Other,
white hands
wrap tight about,
thickening
your viewpoint.

A sable tip
striking indulgently
against something
that might be paper,
might be skin,
or even your slight
anticipatory in-breath.

Take that mark,
carry it about
during the day
and in the night,
touch it faintly
with the permissive whorl
of your index finger.

In the sea
that is her tongue,
in the instant
you approach,
there is
surrender.

In the time taken
to tilt your head this way
and then back again,
your eyelids close
creating a sonic boom
of potential.

All this as you hesitate
at the door, thinking

*maybe*
*now*
*maybe*
*Now*
*She will*
*let me*
*Enter...*

The table
is set.
Step over
the threshold.

## translation more dear than idea

Thought
extrudes degenerating desire.
Language walks outside the delineations
of Ink.
Above Film,
Language hesitates
on green screen projection,
a superimposing calibration
of what might have been
a trance gate.
Language poses as saviour to thought
and grows nearer to Ink.
interceding between
the conflicted lexicons
of odd centipedal connections,
Language commands Ink.
Ink buries itself in earth's
Narrative

## imprints from Rosewater

in the course of suspension
  over
in the act of lowering
  down
in the ritual that is burying
  under

time becomes staggered images
of someone else's life, bleeding
frames over your bitter green.

everywhere you uncover
a double exposure,

the thought that you
  could
have been them
    could
have been caught

in a faultless Vonnegut jump
broken over a Dali sunrise
to find Picasso reading the soft, wet
tea leaves in your evolving cup.

your fingers are pushing into
the clay of tomorrow's dawn

> *remember me*
> *call my name*
> *one more time*
> *define me*
> *refine me*
> *inter me*

until the
  tock  ing
    tick  ing
hits the bedrock
of unforgiv  ing craft.

## Saccadic Plunge

An almost time
in the pause
from REM to REM,
a few words were told me
about the deep universe,
the one that fell from the sky
while dull and reticent people
hid their failure behind blinds.

*In the streets outside,*
*life grieves between*
*substantial decay.*
*Those that swim in the past*
*dive down to touch*
*phantom coins of prospect,*
*eyes vulnerable*
*to the spectacle of remorse.*
*These ones fill their lungs*
*with the oxygen*
*of a contrived identity,*
*until the waters clear*
*and the swimmers emerge*
*beside the cornerstones*
*of abandoned buildings.*
*Skittering sight finds*
*that someone*
*has left a door open*
*dinner, on the floor.*

We all leave like this,
hurried and unaware,
the river rising
up the steps
to greet us.
And there is no ferry,

only submergence
into recollection,
every measure of us
vibrating.

## wake up, fall

it is tougher
in the white of white
where i observe
unfathomable black
in sounding depths
a secchi disc iris sinks
into the astounding
ligament laughter
i find indecisiveness
in a deeper trance
piano keys cartwheel
along leather strop
and it becomes
a welcome mat
for hyped up anthems
of morning addiction
white pours out black
radiation rises
from the rougher
complexities
of insight

## rings and keys

late the other night
city rumbling
underground
you sat by the light
of a solitary screen
and found the power
you thought had left
found it firmly set
in your hands
your fingertips flying
along the keyboard
a potent circle
eased its way along you
finding just the right place
to rest its weight
your thoughts
breathing over
an ember rousing
in your belly
traveling your spine
up to your hands
reaching out
through your fingertips
as they searched the keys
for the right curves and angles
to express the electric surge

it seems harder now
tighter in the lines
and the weight sets you sighing
here in the early morning
that breaks over the screen
touching your strength
an ancient mystery uncoiling
in the palms of your hands

## white noise from the hidden whore

she claims she comes from
under the emergency room table
she calls out in some distress
at the expectations fisting their way
like big mother-goddess implications
unfortunate dancing
she welcomed
a robbery of suspicious rides
Oh how Virginia shivers
voracious for the blade
in the far corner
she burns in the aftershock
of pale music leaking from
mouths hanging slack
whispering rape and murder
and birthing
the beautiful spaces
where those things
miraculously occur

## white noise from fellini

he is such a beautiful man
if only they would beat him
he could find himself again
somewhere
under their hardened faces
in the language of ashes
he found
his/her tongue
when they kissed
the sound of drowning trees
the certain collapse of underpinning
he/she lay three circles to his left
discrete, incomplete
and marked in the fluids
of sacrificial animals
offal twisting
under the question of whether
to bless the hermaphrodite's skin
the itch that never abates
in the dust storm he watches
the minotaur run the carnal labyrinth
and witnesses the bastard offspring
of history and laughter
bamboo, willow, leather, wire
all the lashes will not firm him
he weeps
he wails
and the whores look away, wise

## Filtering Hunter S

Splattering reality from both sides,
or maybe three
in the lower tracks of the
smart outsider.
A vandalism of laughter
mocks the broken night,
  agonizing insights
    potentially destructive
      entirely seductive
        menacing in frequency.
Leary,
we have been paralyzed,
there is no enlightened mat
to sit on.
We feel blood flowing out
from between our legs as we fuck.
To negate this illustration
of the Dead American Dream,
we are consciously pushing
the limits of the reptile brain.
It is breaking down,
transcribed through the
radiator of a Cadillac.
Paradise is savage, awake,
an anal ballet of technological madness.
Your rent is unpaid,
the neighbor's wife gets laid
and you hear it all through the walls.
A bloodless patriot
riding the waves of the crisis
after the crisis before
nature hits you straight
with her lines.

Progress goes
  off the chart
    off the record
      off the wall.
Gonzo,
you are fingering the edge
of the razor
and life goes off
with a bang.

# i (?)

i have inverted and bowed
until the small eye
has curved into question.

in capsizing there is seeking
of that which moves behind
in surprised dismissal
of everything  created
since breach.

on the wave
of promised spine,
Pandora places all
that is left of hope
and watches
as it is carried
into desert places.

*eternal Spring of Silent Solitude*

I have distorted reflection
until the question is broken,
and all that *was* created
is brought to disarray.

I have given mySelf
to creativity and found only
Pandora's fingerprints
on my stilled, parched lips.

## Walking With Holly and Jackie

Over flying colours,
the somewhere hopeful
digging
six-foot dreams
into uneasy dusk.

Morphine manners matter
here in the front seat,
driving life through
red lights chased by locked doors
and androgyny's sirens.

Leaving with Lou,
under roaches and ashes,
the night before discords.

The smell on your hands.
  The stain on your thighs.
    The distant rumble loses itself.

Doo, doo, doo....

# Others' Light

## Unseen

I want to know why you limp,
why your lips hang slack
in crooked acceptance of
something you have shadowed.

Hung in the brown,
your optic ornaments
sway with silent truths.

I want to know why you wear
Prussian blue against grey,
why you feign to smile,
stubs yellowed in weighty clasp
of your snarled fingers.

I want to know these things
but I won't ask you.
No, I would not stop you
as you, 45 degrees, slant by,
I so 90 degrees in life.

## Trope and Kisses

I am half awake
You are half asleep

You perceive this
to be identical

I am flowing out
You are flowing in

I surge, You rescind
in-between aftermaths

I am half awake
You are half asleep

years later, accustomed
and oddly metaphorical.

## optique

you tell me to take
my fingers
and thrust them

thus

quickly in my eyes

this sets me looking
inward
at my own inverted
perception

my vision sets me
straight
regarding images
life has hidden

you, superficially stare

as

crimson prints
your puzzled face

## White Rabbit Reversal

I am up out of it all—
you deluge down,
return grainy and flickering.

I am adjusting focal length and aperture—
you are stereographic stuttering,
snapped, alphabetic justifications.

I see no correlations,
no anxious fulcrum.

Set this opposition reeling
with polar attraction.

The nostalgic redemption
of transformed contentment.

## Cicada and Clover

I am small and my hands are far away.
I can't keep up on the trail
that winds its way to the dock.
You are running, running...

I trip over roots and my knees are bleeding.
Dirt-speckled streams of red
flow down my bare legs.
You are still running...

I am alone in the dirt.

Cicada whine pitching my head
into summer's oblivious heat.
There is nothing to do
but pick stones from my wounds.

You don't come back.

The sun descends, I rise,
aching limbs quivering.
I pick purple clover blooms
and suck out their nectar
as I find my own way
to water's edge.

You aren't there,
but I see your footprints.
Leading into the lake,
they disappear...

## Fugitive

Your face, a white clay
smear, screams by
on shuddering rails
that hold you to
your objective.

*pennywisepenny*
*jump the rails*
*runaway take me*
*take me runaway*
*rail the jumps*
*wisepennywise*

I am railway-tied and tracked,
hurtling eastward, flat-green,
tracing faint white lines
on the window –
remnants of your passing.

## The Sorry Dark

In the sorry dark,
I cover you as you sleep
with layers of leaves and sticks
to muffle your complaints.

On my pillow,
wasp words writhe.
They await my falling body
so they might creep stinging
into my ears and mouth.

I see their compounded visions.
They consume the paper
of this blood and bone contract,
and regurgitate it, creating
a gray casket hung over our life.

You are the day stalker.
Great strides on the ridges
take you away from the fungus bed.
Your mouth unhinges and you lick
silver tracks on the open sky.

I am the crevice dweller.
I leave behind my fingernails
as I pull my way up the mountain side.
Each nail grows roots and blooms
a finger-petalled outrage.

In the orange hours you recline.
You complain of time's curve,
as I cover myself again
in the paper of sorry dark.

## Cadaver Rock

Don't be delicate with me, Darling.
Crack open the next cranial chocolate box,
feed me the end of the world.

Melting pure over your fingers.
Let me lick each infinitely despairing moment
off your skin. What is this sin?

Indeterminate remorse. Perfect
as the perfectly circular blisters
beading your beautifully blank lips.

My acceptance astounds you.
Darling, not the green shock of you
– it was the high cliff of mind.

Chalk bare as dazzled Dover.
How could I do anything
but overstep the boundary of you?

At the edges of breathing, after the fall,
this is all there is. My sweet, stained lips
and your mouth, luminous with Japanese lanterns.

## viva voce

foreknowledge
is never enough
inside my mouth
are languages
you cannot hear

I put you gently
between my lips
pull you in slowly
deep into the wet
and warmth

so that you might
understand
these words
I cannot say

so that you might
discover
what you will never
be able to tell

## Matinee

In exposed isolation I am reticent.

The saddled sunlit days are burned into my memory,
and the sighs of my arched moments discarded.
This is a formulaic life, each unforgiving detail
mapped and pinned with strict precision.

Dissolve me, let me flow away in rain, plead
with liquid cries to the moving current.
Take this soul, disperse it so that I never again
feel such a tired smile upon my lips.
I placed it there for your convenience,
for forgiveness, for completion of the circle,
the one that tightens its looped lies as you dance
with the woman in the corner.

Her tilted head offers up moist lips.
You take them and keep your seal of receiving,
so that I may see where you have been.
Her scent is on your face where she rode,
and you, lapping joy, brought to trembling
her thighs about your neck.

I watch as you roll out of the sheets,
clothe yourself in fidelity and a receptive mask.
I am as unresponsive as a threatened possum
as you lick my lips and plead love's lies.
You take my hand and crush the spring blooms
I was going to put in the bedroom.

I let them fall, as you pull me down again.

## Coax

There is the One finger,
single tap
the pointed one.

      Two finger walks path,
      cleft rider twins
      the doubled night.

            Three centered on one,
            leaning fire
            the tripod falling

      Four finger cannot grasp,
      writhes wanting
      the filled void.

Five finger cups nest,
takes time
the bird is held.

            Hand sings to me.

## purblind

...not)

stain of seed at back of throat, bruises
left by fingers' passion, shine
of sweat on naked skin

palms curving waist cannot define
lines taken in hard times, lie of lying,
release displaced

       you are fooled, i am not.

your disgrace, misplaced intelligence
you regress and impress little.

       your moments,

lemon juice to page, visible in split-second
scorch, fleeting expression

       you fear blood.

liquid pressed from harvest,
fermented intoxicating pleasure
wrung from vine and branch,

in your veins
       the echo of self-delusion
in your room
       an exquisite moan
in your life
       diminished sight

(IT is...

## sensual scarification

your quick, paper cut
      kisses
pattern me, trails ripe
      red.
tongue whipped, willingly
      tied
by these bindings that will not
      break.

raw response to blistering
      caress.

flesh to marrow
      undressing
my skin to yours
      sewing
sinew to sweat
      sharing
sutured regrets
      dissolving

the scars of our uncertain
      success.

*I am sustained by this—*

your iron
      lung

our lingering
      kiss.

## What Remains

I choose
the short and simple words
to make this point,
that somewhere
among your lonely thoughts
this poem is all there is,
nothing more than a single note,
if one is to be honest

some flat or sharp,
dropped from Eleanor's face
when you took photographs
trying to steal a part of time
you knew would not last.

Your kiss smells of gasoline,
you wait at the torn backdoor
for some undiscovered spark
to set you aflame,
to give you the pain
that lets you know love
might still be a living thing.

You hope to leave some scent
that lingers after the photographs
are ashes,
this too goes away,
with one draw-out vowel
that sounds something
like "o."

## Prone to Smoking

This is the wrinkled tobacco
you left drying on my kitchen table
during the second month.

You wept, as I stopped on the rails
of your speeding pen, and so inked
you predictably won the prize.
Later, drunk, you navigated away
to conceal the diary
of your oversleeping love.

With blood, these years are preserved
and I forgive you for outliving me.
You are the jinx on my lips –
I cannot afford even half
of the verbiage you spill
over my naked body.

My tongue is as thick
as wood, and the hum
of memory deafens me.

I will never know what
you threw out or what recycled.
Your past and recent conquests,
pretty ones slumbering
in the burn of your cumbersome will.

Lines on the page define
the limits of my importance.

This year, you are solvent,
hoarding recollections
and hurtling legalities
into the fire.

## Discourse and Discord

This is the last dynamic touch
before you shift to static,
white noise Orpheus.

A salt lick, a crumb trail,
unending age of lessons,
still you look back.

Your nature is
a moody organism's
shedding, hallucinatory skin.

You left your former self
across my bedsheets.

I saw you riding
punishment's storm.
You had forgotten
you were alive.

You kissed me with
the folded gray whisper
of my chosen name.

You could not have known
I would consume it.

A maenad's retribution.

Reality
is your afflicted lyre,
you drone the chords
of distorted time.

Your misplaced faith, tragically sung.

## something like a still life

*how*

you found in the market
the one thing you needed
for that particular day,
purchased it at a price
you deemed practical
wrapped it in delicate tissues
placed it in one of those bags
with the accelerated rate
of decomposition,
so that even the packaging
would be momentary.

*how*

the rows upon rows
of flowers made you remember
the large packages of crayons
only other children got,
the ones with all the metallic tones
the ones allowing you to colour
not only every currency
but every tone of flesh
you could imagine touching
and possessing.

*I leave you*

in the confines of your covert room,
broken bowls of stolen moments
and trinket obsessions
clinging to you in the darksmall
of fractured sleep.
you accumulate in a silken sow's ear
the superficial moments
of your tiny, tedious life

*now.*

## The Pro and The Con

It is the suspension of day.

He pronounces to me
he is close to the end
and needs to read
and I must listen.
His hands rest on
the base of my spine.
He questions if I have
anything open,
anything significant
open (am I not so?)

I sit very straight,
*palms up,*
not in the manner
that springs to the minds
of those always searching.
Not a display
of meditative distortion.
I think to myself,
*that* is the image
presented by the fickle
who, having no concept
of their Id-entity and
presenting themselves as
In-the-Know, offer
the posture of poseur.
No, nothing like that.
*This, my upturning,*
is in anticipation of the
feminine dirge
that will inevitably fall
into my cupped hands.

His words emerge,
gliding notions
of masculine blessing.
- *blessing*
another concept
coveted and damaged
by the dubiously enlightened.
Never trust someone
who tells you
they have path in(sight).
*blessing indeed* –
he is handing me
my chosen sorrows!

My fingertips
press into the scar
of our joining,
knowing behind it
there are fireflies
high on poppy-red
spilling from his tongue.
I know that this
is how we master Babel.

He removes his hands.
Time is now capricious.
I note a repeating
in the evening call,
orbital as a noose.
Foretelling tightens
in the story he delivers.
In it, she becomes a martyr
never whispering
what she sees
on the precipice

of what is breathing
and what may not be.

He moves close,
his lips touching
the curve of my ear,
and unsettled, says to me
that I *am* open,
*so astonishingly open.*

In my eye's dilation,
he is irrelevant.

## Permutation

I think perhaps you should reconsider your position.
Precarious on the precipice sitting
and that point you made must have punctured
something vital.

Don't recall the scene snowbound.
Ice storms and frozen time are settling in a glass globe
that shakes palsy-pure in your crooked house.

I see that now.

All the corners are acute
and you bluster up some coughing bag
through obdurate fists.

Up, up, up!

Away it goes yelping
a jolted, lagging tune
carried on scorched tongues.

Out the throat of yesterday it leaps,
to land pulsing here beside the smears
my worn-down finger nubs have made.

Red is in fashion this season
and I bleed for you.

From your position, this seems only fair.

## At the Moment, Only I

I indulge a stranger,
embrace their
mind
and count all the steps
to an obliterated foundation.

I write a page
of in-between-the-lines,
gifting the now
with trampled revelations.

You present to me
a tunneled sunlight
emitting inaccuracies
posing as truth.

We stumble here
and impossibly there
along indistinct pathways,
our progress smudged.

You drive me into a horizon
of thickened time
so that we might expire
with mutterings of pretense.

We are an arrested interest.

We denounce the lowered
window shades which hide
our indifferent embrace.

We retreat intuitive,
slightly thirsty
for elapsed green love
and in deepest dark
our fingers part
releasing living sand
into our-glass half empty.

And we kiss, never touching.

## Whole has Hole Inside

*Darling,*

Again press these thick, foetal grubs between
my lips.  Gift me with uncertain, scarring acceptance,
meted out in doses without sight.

Salt me down the flushed sides of my face,
painting the disgraceful beauty of our sudden

contra(diction)

inevitable
    divisible
        mercy

in one pupated kiss

a sentience
        half
        promised,

neglect
        never
        complete.

## As Much As Necessary

*"Grief's never had it so good."*
*- Susan Musgrave, "Here it Comes - Grief's Beautiful Blowjob"*

i.

He is starting to figure it out.

He is ready to explode.  His words,
the thin lines of blushing light, out of his
becoming, out of his lips, he breathes
rain into the complaint of her silent moments.
He holds the egg of her love in his dreaming
hands and urges her to push, urges her to
push, just once more.

ii.

He doesn't know what it is,
what comes through him –
the idea of this perhaps,
   through the writing
      through the sharing
         through the steam of
a coffee-ringed memory.
In some ways, it is that part
of himself left behind that stains.

iii.

Of the darkness.
In the numbers.
In the eyes of the forest
sleeping, there is the warning
of laid-back ears.
His anger.
Her wondering.
The empty and emotionless
fucking,

followed by dreamless sleep
and always, always
the hunger.

iv.

She knows every integer
that weeps itself to the next.
The hope of her mouth is
a dropped penny in
well-wishing starvation.
She releases the bloom
of a black sheep wounded,
spilling garnet pollen
over the loveless street.

v.

Closed, closed...
She is hiding
the chattering of her
teeth
and under the thin skin
of tattooed joy,
she is conquered
by one simple truth,
Open, open...

vi.

He says it will be interesting,
takes his fist and slams it
into the air of her flesh,
a union almost sexual, yet more.
Her head is filled with magic,
the refuse of his cowardice,
the host of her tomorrow.

He says it will be interesting,
and she wants very badly to agree.

vii.

She goes slowly,
goes very slowly,
so she can relish the stitches
of her rising day, the herding of
her uncertain future.  Her mouth opening,
tearing threads that held her silent.  In urgent
explosion

the sun rises between her lips.

## nihil ad rem

Compose for me
a wronged feature
of returning compulsion.

You are a bored Braille gunner.

You face the frightening orbit
of your limited understanding.

And in this vision I have
        of you
as a tiny god

I am the remains
        of a life
you cannot pursue.

There is no face
        or body
to be remembered
        or buried.

There is something though,
returning to touch you

in a
very
limited
form.

## Silent Resonance

Early spring –

the water is cold.
You place your hands
upon it, palms open,
flat, as if to float
upon the surface of life.

This sea –
your life, my life...

all the space between,
invisible, an infinite
expansion,

breathtaking catastrophe.

Along the shore,
you commune, half-despairing
the flesh that holds you in,
wanting to step
out of demanding skin...

To what then?
What is there but this?

Know this is you.

Dimensionless, your fingers
trace the places where life
walks, salvage
the scarred answers,

speak the syllables which
existed before sound,

the truth between breaths.

Palms wet,
I hold each side
of your face, beg you to
dissolve,

there is no between...
only here, only this,

your inhale, my exhale

We hunger for effortless language,
stumble over nouns and verbs
that define nothing.

This pantomime repeats,
our invention, our excuse,
a closing act where most fall
gluttonous on indolent pitches,

empty promises of accidental touch.

Elsewhere,
beyond definition
we wheel as one.

I touch
my palms to
water, leaving

your fingerprints.

## Fisher Man

Come closer,
I will fill your mouth
with cedar smoke
and paint black circles
about your eyes.

Here, by the river,
I lie on the gravel,
watch as you cast
your line into the current.

You are fishing again.
Always trying new bait,
seeking
a shiny one in the water.

I see you arch your back,
and easily play out
that tempting morsel.
Each concentric circle
is a promise of pleasure.

A hook, a line
and all my time
spent in the rocks.

You let me keep the
skin and bones.
I make them into
images of you.
I put them on the table
when you are gone.

They taste of oil and death.

## Down the River

I will not go down
the river today
I will stay
in sheltered brush
hide my soul
from ripping wind
hide my face
from blistered day
hide my heart
from knife current.

Down the river
He walks
steeltoed boots
bloodstained hands
He speaks leather lashings
He sells fractured lies
He buys split futures
to divide up
like pillaged goods
from a hanged man's pockets.

Down the river
where nothing begins
down the river
where nothing breathes
He has built a den
of antler and skins
cast-offs and remnants
bound together
with spit and mud.

He waits for me

I have enclosed myself
in willow branches
beside the river.

I will not go down.
I will not go down.

## Of Eggs and Dogs

Her day peels back
like a hard-boiled egg.
She drips through the room,
wide, red apple eyes,
castanet lashes,
quivering thighs clenched shut.
Her step, delicate as fingernails
across dusty blackboard.

She speaks bees.
Honey lingers on the arch
of her lips,
the wax seals her throat.
There is no exhale.
Not today.

Dogs speak to her
when sunrise splinters.
Promises of buried bones.
The rain barrel is overflowing.
Heavy hands brush away
her egg-white tears.
The dogs call her
into the woods.
She runs.

## Carl

Being Carl is curse enough.
He despises me.
He despises you.
He delays the lines
regardless of your needs
or mine.

He says he has to leave.
He travels home by subway
and step by step he breaks down.

His homecoming is complicated.

Fishing for cold plates
in the refrigerator,
he is convinced God
is snacking on his leftovers.

*He* is the loaves.
*He* is the fishes.

Denied.
Hoarded.

## Margin Call

His ammonia signature
is scrawled in narrow places,
where life is carried, boxed
and sorted, grime of the times.

Dumpster dreamer,
his ochre fingers claw
with gnawed nails at the
tear tab of liquid release.

He of scattered mind,
facts, figures, in disarray,
Wall Street Journal dreams
of his clear, pinstriped days

before –

worm-holes wind careless
through his Uptown dance,
rabbit-ears-down-the-hole
chittering tablets, lost laws,
dabbing his blue-chip tears
with silken remainders.

## Latte with my Lad

I could not have imagined
you so tall,

whose shoes I try to fill,
and cannot.

Your stride is longer than mine
yet you still look to me,

though covertly now, lest peers
peer at us through coffee shop windows.

You want my canvas coat,
the one army-green that matches my

Converse sneakers.
"Nobody else's Mum wears those," you say.

Conversant, we sit, and I
seek your eyes,

your hands are bigger than mine,
you drink a latte and laugh when

I say this is easier than when
I brought you here in a stroller,

and it is in some ways,
but in others

growing pains me more
than I can bear.

## Elizabeth

She wouldn't write it,
right it.

Sorrow caught
in the magpie branches,

thoughts planting themselves
into the soil of Scottish ages.

Hills and lonely moors,
the heads of slaughtered swine,

tongues wagging cold
in tiny butcher shops,

nowhere near Burns' light.
Ashes about the doorstep

pattern a memory
of thistle gone to seed

blown so very far
across the Atlantic.

## Dearest Isabel
*for Isabel da Silva*

Dearest Isabel,
I am in the tarnish of cloud we sought.
I am walking in the seaside graveyard.
I wander only the edge where the
questionable are buried,  their bones
crumbling at the same rate as the nuns
resting higher up.  Sisters cradled together
in encouraged sisterhood, seeking to define
viewpoint even in death.

There are no postcards to send from here,
no tiny stones to pick up and send to you, my
Dearest Isabel, only this small vial of soil for
  your art
    your life
      your breath.
Though you disappear for years at a time,
no one knows me
the hidden ways you do,
in my tarnish of cloud,
Dearest Isabel.

## Emily

Emily's perfection
skips across the school yard,
Mary Janes scuffed,
white stockings unable to hide
the scabs on her knees.

Tumbling double-dutch
trips to hoop
and four-square fascinations.

Chalk-smear-kisses
hopscotch
across Red Rover passing.

Her London Bridges
are falling quickly
and twist as maple-key-copters.

Emily's perfection
is captured
and her future folded
carefully
in a crumpled paper crane.

## Dolly

Dolly is made of twigs,
weeps beaded blue
kisses,  matchstick lips
arch the hiss of home fires
black smudged down your
shoulder blades to sudden fade.

She is paralytic perfect,
Raggedy heart beating
in the deep white,
filled with pills and panic,
a silenced confection
embalmed in spice.

Dolly holds curved promises,
walks in circles to remember
the strings tied about her
fingers, so tight, tight, and
all her fables written in Braille.

She meets you
in four-walled places,
her crooked seams
bleed wet aphrodisiac
on the panting carpet,
de-clawed magnolia cat.

Dolly spreads sweet
on the drumming couch,
1920's furs and bobbed glory,
oxblood marked, she
pumps hips in your
iron lung confessional.

She is the soft anonymous
talker in your chest
pulling the string that
makes you speak,
squeezing the one thing
you thought inaccessible.

Dolly tells you there is no end to it.
You set a fire and believe her.

## anahata

*for Jaime Shea*

she was thinking of a flower
with twelve green petals,
each one pointing to
the hours of her Day
passing in swift succession.

not enough time
to hold the infinite blades
of summer grass
between her fingers.

she calls to the children
who run barefoot
along the riverside.

she was thinking of a flower
with twelve green petals,
each one an expression
of singular life.

twelve petals falling,
each alone
in the footprints to Home.
there, she folded herself
onto the porch swing

and the children danced,
showering her
with all the petals
she could not find
on her own.

## Samuel

sensing himself
the obscure son
of a profane mother
he embraces blue turmoil
and the brief curiosities
of his terminal disease
sensing heritage
as something
to be buried
he pants
hot fascination
at this torment
and condemnation
his empty hearth
births a universe
of angel-ridden
black holes
the future of
his reality
a single leaf of paper
a consonant
written cautiously
with trembling hand

## Because the air is full of words that start with "i"

He tells you he found it
in the air, plucked and ate it,
yet remained unconvinced.

You want to tell him that
the air
is little more than his breath.

He wants to know where
to find more, more to run
his fingers among, to pick
and consume, to fill all the
spaces he believes exist.

You want to tell him that he must
devour himself,
must become the ouroboros cliché.

You open your notebook.
You pick up your pen.

He thinks you will draw him
a map of all the sunken islands
beyond the shores of his perception.

You begin this way,
with a vertical line
and end somewhere
at the top, though
separated,
with a small point
that says:

*You end where*
*all things end,*

*you end with*
*the beginning.*

You hand him the paper.

He examines the marks.
He calls you puzzling.
You agree.

## Gaston

Gaston is organizing his funding
the only way he can think of –
a constancy of tips and loose change,
accounting for his activity in complete
spreadsheet consistency.

Gaston rummages through wastebaskets,
through the refuse bins behind the bank,
turns his pockets inside out
looking for that order he once had.
The bottom line has dropped out
and he finds himself in free fall.

His mind is collapsing as he counts
each crack on the sidewalk.
Time tocks, talks, tocks
in the back of his brain.
He is seeking dropped coinage
and someone else's past.

Gaston wants to steal
the lines of their fingerprints
so he may have something
resembling adequate identification.

## To You Who Hesitated

Whoever you are, wherever,
spying me through auto window

catching your own
sorrowful reflection
and passing it hot,
like this or that,
back to me,
reversed, rehearsed.

I'm writing this for you,
as you tie laces
making safety
your first concern.

I can't comprehend why, why,
why, you chose this place
to share apprehension.

mid-road traveler.
yellow line straddler

cautionary as road kill –

## In Any Language, Fall

In arch parody,
under blackened thumb,
the General orders the birth
of spring.

Green punches through
the dust of orphaned land
and children gnaw on the sweet,
shining sugar
of their family's blood.

In the palace, the General
thinks of four-star blossoms
and the deflowering
of knotted cages not quite ready
for consumption.

On a bed of paper lace, his boots
leave muddy tracks, hard-lashed
and streaming with ruptured promise.

The birds mimic spring.

In a bare room, the General hears
his name called out

*(his mother
 his death)*

The little breath of Fall
hangs sharp over his neck

he feels unexpectedly weak.

## James, Giving Way

James is taking account
in a time of convinced failing.
He thinks she will seize every item
he carefully put away.
All she leaves is a note
on his doorway to morning,
fragments of meaning.

He is reading the floorboards,
the red and white of misery
(as hers not his).
James is vacant, obvious,
has somehow woven authenticity
to clothe each delusion.

He presses his hand tight
around two ancient coins,
released economy of emotion.

He says it is better to buy that kind of thing.

His collapsed childhood is re-enacted
in the manner he pours milk into a mug,
the way he denies toast its butter,
words he habitually repeats.

The past is never cleaned out,
it is there under his fingernails,
captured while he tried to

*hang on—*

(let go, James)

## Bloodied Betty

The sun, stretched taut
as a deerskin drum,
beat its path across the day.
Bloodied Betty, the oracle,
mumbled unheard,
her faded feet stepping
over cracked ways.

One eye hushed, fogbound
in the mists of to-be,
Betty sings strong like
cold salt water,
rattling bones left
in dead men's boats.
She has the buried voice.

A lazy swaying of sight
sent her far out
to fly with petrels.
Distant souls, a covenant
weeping salt pillars
and absorbing life,
float face up, gazing.

Betty paints with a simple
diseased brush the lines
where  the cudgel is taken up.
The cull of the inconvenient.
The bleeding runs along gutters
and is swept careless into ocean.

Under her tattered hood,
Bloodied Betty clicks her tongue.
Ancient Birdspeak,
an intangible memento.

Raven listens with reverence,
eyes tracking the symbols
made by Betty's knotted hands.

One tired breath out and
Raven stretches his wings.
Betty slumps.
Blood thickens at her feet.
The sun beats blue
the tired face of night

## D&C

     *"Please Mummy, please…"*
She can't read them by
herself
She in size 2 true shoe
she still can't count
she'll never reach size 10
     *"when? when? when?"*
And now
please
is no longer
a plea
while rocking in the arms
of natal(ess)
emptiness
     *womb/tomb*
she skipped everything
to have only this
empty nest
     *she felt it move*
     *she did, she did*
     *she felt it move*
     *as it died*
half-waking to her legs
splayed
masked cuckoos
over her fleshy nest
scraping out the
vestiges
and she wonders aloud
why she is awake
     *Drug her*
     *Drug her down*
     *Drug her to drown*
in this
amniotic sea of loss

size 2, true
she'll never hit 10
I'm reading the lies
    *"When Mummy, when?"*

## Donald Waits in the Hall

Donald turned eighty last year.
This year, they forgot him in the hall,
eighty-one being unceremonious
and not containing what they hoped for,
his wronged manuscripts,
his crumpled will,
his death.

Donald imagines being stopped,
root of his breath cut short,
lips unable to reach the oxygen
which may or may not exist,
he can't tell and he hopes
it will evade him.
The bark of his body
is far too thick for
any of this to
matter.

Donald turned eighty-one this year.
He asked why Ezra Pound
was still not free, his own vision,
not unlike pale petals, blurring by.
They forgot to check
his wet, black
breath.

Donald seeks to simplify his death
and waits patiently for Ezra
to write to him with the
images of his passing,
and as he waits,
life petrifies
his lungs.

## time is measured in drops

she is
precisely pale
curled and refined
in a west coast way
her amber breath
questioning how it is she
managed to get here
this place where bags
of something unreal
burn their way
into the veins
of people like her
faint, wondering people
who find themselves
one day less certain
of where they might be
in ten years
she examines her hair
unsure
how long it will remain
she is quite transient
a rapid blush intensifies
her hushed lips
and she glances upwards
to see if time
is passing
still

## 15 minutes of...

1.

access me to excess
gorge on my

obvious
nature

here where a lemon
is quite simply

unfortunate
fruit

and there is nothing
hidden in

the
seeds

and the peel is
certainly not

captured
sunlight.

2.

You thought I said
oracular membrane.

I did not.

I only whispered
ocular membrane,
thinking you would see

more clearly, if you
noticed it there
and removed it.

I discovered

that you wanted
me to see for you,
while you suckled
on a foreign tongue.


3.
After
i knew you
better
i knew you
Before

and though you whispered
with familiarity into my ear

Before
i knew you
better
i knew you
After

4.
they said to hold it
together

double sided tape
flesh to fabric

a cleavage caged
pushed to blooming

they said hold it
together

and he said
it was wasted tape

5.

from every pore
and every vein
from every artery
for every pain
visions of sugar
feeling high
racing hot red
from needle
to thigh

6.

complacent
and vacant

she dressed herself
to acceptable levels

each button
   just so
each buckle
   just so
each lace

all fatigued nakedness

covered

a costuming of social
graces

distant wildness
refined

she wore
a weary look

of acceptance

vacantly complicit

## Production Made

He can't figure it out.

The void hits him.
He flinches at the sound
of a slamming trailer door.

She offers him a costume,
a hand, and touches him,
implying intimacy.

He saw this before,
when his cat placed a paw
on him, signifying ownership.

In the trailer, her laughter
explodes across the mirror.

He watches her stroke
her likeness, can't
comprehend the seduction.

He does not know
where to drive
his cravings.

In this impulsive
separation,
in the dread of
disapproval,
he is exquisitely

abandoned.

# Baby Doll

*"Excuse me, Mr. Vacarro, but I wouldn't dream of
eatin' a nut that a man had cracked in his mouth."*
– Tennessee Williams, Baby Doll

Baby Doll plays dress-up
in her husband's house,
walks past him and lets him smell
the possibility of owning her.
These are the games she likes,
hide-and-seek virgin, she knows
that the sweetest sweat
comes from a man waiting.

Outside, the cotton gin
criticizes the southern sky
and Baby Doll's skin,
finer than the finest fabric,
flushes hot at foreign touch.
She pushes away, knowing
that here, even the coolest
well has energy to burn.

Baby Doll sleeps in the last
furnished room, her womb
unbroken.  She believes there are
ghosts in the house and they
resent her, as she fears them,
and all of this sagging prison.

Her husband is blazing, he has
lost his hold and finds bullets
speak clearest of all.

Baby Doll has signed away
his crimes with her attic name.
Her warm tongue moves across
her chaste lips and she waits
to be remembered, or forgotten.

## Charles

Charles is trying
to get it right
he wants to liberate
all men
from the foundation
of women's legs
and all the traps
found between
apron strings and purrs
Charles sees it as
a hole to fall into
he takes a drink
and clutches his balls
thinking how liberating
is his own hand

## oblique prayer

emma cannot be
composed
she injects capacities
of life
hits back
in self-destructive    exposé
smacks
over the edge
one hand irregular
in sorrow
her man
concerned about
her sanity
finds comfort in a bed
of differing    grace
like a nun
emma worships him

## Ivor and Leslov

Ivor and Leslov face each other
over hot coffee.
They talk with urgency
and no little substance.

Ivor says, *"No, no! It wasn't like that at all!*
*There was snow that year*
*and the roads closed.*
*We had to sleep in*
*the railyard. Don't you*
*remember?"*

Leslov shakes his head. *"No, no!*
*You are wrong. It was the year*
*before,*
*the year Marika began coughing blood*
*and poor little Istvan was lost*
*in the North Woods.*
*Anyway, you were deep in the vodka then,*
*how could you*
*remember*
*any of this?"*

A slide of disgust.
A glance of mistrust.
And finally, the slight twitch that says,
*"Yes, yes. We know each other*
*far too well."*

Silence.

The raising of mugs.

Sometimes,
  you have to forget.

## Countenance

On five calculated tips,
you present the reasons,
each counted to thunderclap,
precisely timed and intractable.
There you paint the failures
set to front exactly so,
a list of omissions.

I fall short.

This trompe l'oeil still wet,
I run my hands down the surface
distorting the perspectives and leaving
fingerprints that decline.
Scrutinizing this spectacle,
I rescind my suggestion
that such flatness can
have depth.

## Forgotten One

Listen
to the footfalls of silence,
they kiss the under-running river,
sharp ice and winter games.

Over the fields of me
rests the horizon of you—
the sun sets heavy
on our unspoken path.

Listen
to the birdsong of silence,
whisper the things you hear
between my invisible lines.

Recall for me now
how we knew each other
before we met.

You always occupy
the within-locked
room of my home.

Listen!

Open the door –
I am the spiral of
all that is silence.

## How Close We Come To Emptiness

She takes the abacus
of regret,
holds still to her lips
the parted thighs
of his distant sorrow,
drinks deep
of his trepidations.

You say he is only human,
sinew you say –
flesh being frail,
but here the sinew
holds together all
you possess.

*This is certainly nothing.*

Nervous reflex
twitches eyelid.
It is a louvered life,
a series of snapshots
witnessing
the trickle of day,
a reflection
of silvered fish
captured as vapour
in war-torn Asia.

*Pretence and predictable details.*

The hand touching
the back of her neck,
here and here.
A mark.
A signature.

Ink spilling down
the vertebral caress.

We find the night
in various states
of disrobing.
All the tea leaves
whisper of remorse.
There is no emperor.

## The Unspoken Light

*No.*

I invent nothing,
seek

nothing,

into this space drop
masked revelations,
twin confrontations of
exacting passions,
budded moments of Venetian
repertoire, marble-white
deception—

I spill,
willingly

bound to you,
heat and stain

tied and trembling,
a shudder of familiar
fascination, your fingers
weaving limitless sanctuary,
historical knots
fondling curls of
rare irradiance,

hesitant never
cherishing the wince

the strain
the pain

each catch of breath
a brink fallen over,
a tumble of cliff death
and shimmering salt,

a command covering
the scent of breasts

taste curled along tongue,
pitch of twenty solar breaths,
mysterious moving,
toss of fleshed bronze
stammering hunger
encountering syllables,
the untying of substitutions
lips pressing
to snake-bitten blooms.

I invent nothing
seek

nothing, break
willingly

stirred by your touch
robbed by your knowledge.

O! in Venice
you gondola thief,
canals of cryptic futures.

Salutary, you ask
if I will stay:

*Yes.*

## stay

so you cannot leave,
i will be brief.

this is only to say that
red
is my favourite colour and that
you
bring it to my cheeks.

if you are still here,
touch them.

Dale Winslow has been an interpretive naturalist, wildlife and fisheries biologist, teacher, editor, publisher, writer, photographer and painter. She resides with her family on Vancouver Island, British Columbia and continues to be interested in pretty much everything. She hopes one day to have her own microscope.

## Acknowledgements

My Gratitude to John Oughton for his excellent editing and to Stephen Roxborough and Milo Duffin for their talent and patience in layout and cover design. Thank you as well to these three wonderful people for their support and friendship.

Many thanks and much love to Si Philbrook, who told me I could and made sure I did.

Thanks to all who lent an ear and encouraged me along the way: William Marshe, Steven Szewczok, Erin Badough, Lance Strate and the vast community of creative people I have had the pleasure to come to know through the internet, many who have become family to me.

Deep thankfulness to my friend Meir Ribalow, who blessed my life with his presence in more ways than I can count. I miss you, Meir.

To my father, Ian, who opened the love of poetry in me and was my rock. To my mother, Barbara, for her never-ending love and incredible spirit. To my husband, Tom, and my sons, Quade and Harper, whose love makes all things possible.

CPSIA information can be obtained at www.ICGtesting.com
Printed in the USA
LVOW12*0047171013

357260LV00003B/3/P